DATE			

ROBIN REDBREAST

ROBIN REDBREAST

AND

OTHER VERSES

BY

WILLIAM ALLINGHAM

PICTURES BY

HELEN ALLINGHAM, KATE GREENAWAY,
CAROLINE PATERSON, AND HARRY FURNISS

Core Collection Books, inc.
GREAT NECK, NEW YORK

First Published in 1887 as
"Rhymes for the Young Folk"
New Edition 1930
Reprinted 1979

International Standard Book Number 0-8486-0007-X

Library of Congress Catalog Number 78-74507

PRINTED IN THE UNITED STATES OF AMERICA

MR. ALLINGHAM'S DEDICATION

TO

GERALD, EVA, AND LITTLE HENRY
AND OTHERS LIKE THEM
THIS BOOKLET
IS LOVINGLY INSCRIBED.

CONTENTS

FAIRIES AND ELVES

INTRODUCTION

WHEN I was a little girl, three poems by William Allingham sang themselves into my memory. You know and love these poems, too—"The Fairies," "Wishing," and "Robin Redbreast."

Which of us knows other child poems by Allingham? Not you; and not I—for years and years.

Last summer, when I was looking over some old picture-books in the Library of Congress, I pulled down from the shelf a thin little red book. I opened it and found—a treasure! "Rhymes for the Young Folk" by Allingham, with illustrations by Kate Greenaway, Helen Allingham, Caroline Paterson, Harry Furniss—verses as lovely as the pictures, pictures as lovely as the verses.

My immediate desire was to share this treasure trove with my friends, and I took the book to The Macmillan Company. They said, at once, that it must go into their Little Library Series. So here are the poems and pictures brought together, for your joy, in this little book.

EDNA TURPIN.

Green Hills, Blue Mountains, Rocks, and
  Streams,
  Birds, Woodland, Starry Night, Sea Foam,
Flowers, Fairies, Children, Music, Dreams,
A Book, a Garden Chair—Sweet Home!

PLAYING ALONE

I SAW A LITTLE BIRDIE FLY

I saw a little birdie fly,
  Merrily piping came he;
"Whom d'ye sing to, Bird?" said I.
  "Sing?——I sing to Amy!"

"Very sweet you sing," I said.
  "Then," quoth he, "to pay me,
Give one little crumb of bread,
  A little smile from Amy."

"Just," he sings, "one little smile;
  Oh, a frown would slay me!
Thanks, and now I'm gone awhile——
  Fare-you-well, dear Amy!"

A SWING SONG

Swing, swing,
Sing, sing,
Here's my throne, and I am a king!
Swing, sing,
Swing, sing,
Farewell, Earth, for I'm on the wing!

Low, high,
Here I fly,
Like a bird through sunny sky;
Free, free,
Over the lea,
Over the mountain, over the sea!

Up, down,
Up and down,
Which is the way to London Town?
Where, where?
Up in the air,
Close your eyes, and now you are there!

Soon, soon,
Afternoon,
Over the sunset, over the moon;
Far, far,
Over all bar,
Sweeping on from star to star!

No, no,
Low, low,
Sweeping daisies with my toe.
Slow, slow,
To and fro,
Slow——
　　　slow——
　　　　　slow——
　　　　　　　slow.

SLEEPING

Do all your sleeping at night,
For then niddy-noddy is right;
    But awake you must keep
    And it won't do to sleep,
In the middle of broad daylight.

The sun at the end of the day
Takes his mighty great candle away;
   A curtain on high
   Is drawn over the sky,
And the stars peep thro' if they may.

There's the curtain of night over all;
There's our own window curtain so small;
   And least in their size,
   Over Emily's eyes
Her fringed little eyelids will fall.

She kneels at the side of her bed,
And softly her prayers are said;
   Now, a kiss, my dear;
   Come, Angels, near,
And keep watch round the little one's bed.

A STRANGE LITTLE DREAM

A strange little dream
On a long star-beam
Ran down from the midnight skies,
To curly-haired Fred
Asleep in his bed,
With the lids on his merry blue eyes.

Under each lid
The thin dream slid,
And spread to a picture inside,
A new world there,
Most strange and rare,
Tho' just by our gardenside.

Rivers and rocks,
And a treasure box,
And floating in air without wings,
And the speaking beast,
And a royal feast——
My chair beside the kings;

A land of flowers,
And of lofty towers
Carved over in marble white
With living shapes
Of panthers and apes
That gambol in ceaseless flight;

And a cellar small
  With its cave in the wall
Stretching many a mile underground!
  And the rope from the moon!——
  Fred woke too soon,
For its end could never be found.

WISHING

Ring-ting! I wish I were a primrose,
A bright yellow primrose blowing in the
　　　spring!
　The stooping boughs above me,
　The wandering bee to love me,
The fern and moss to creep across,
　　And the elm tree for our king!

Nay—stay! I wish I were an elm tree,
A great lofty elm tree, with green leaves gay!
　The winds would set them dancing,
　The sun and moonshine glancing,
The birds would house among the boughs,
　　And sweetly sing!

17

Oh—no! I wish I were a robin,
A robin or a little wren, everywhere to go;
  Through forest, field, or garden,
  And ask no leave or pardon,
Till Winter comes with icy thumbs
    To ruffle up our wing.

Well—tell! Where should I fly to,
Where go to sleep in the dark wood or dell?
  Before a day was over,
  Home comes the rover,
For Mother's kiss—sweeter this
    Than any other thing!

AMY MARGARET

Amy Margaret's five years old,
Amy Margaret's hair is gold,
Dearer twenty-thousand-fold
   Than gold, is Amy Margaret.

"Amy" is friend; is "Margaret"
The pearl for crown or carcanet?
Or peeping daisy, Summer's pet?
   Which are you, Amy Margaret?

A friend, a daisy, and a pearl;
A kindly, simple, precious girl—
Such, howsoe'er the world may twirl,
  Be ever, Amy Margaret!

THE BUBBLE

See, the pretty planet!
   Floating sphere!
Faintest breeze will fan it
   Far or near;

World as light as feather;
   Moonshine rays,
Rainbow tints, together,
   As it plays;

Drooping, sinking, failing,
   Nigh to earth,
Mounting, whirling, sailing,
   Full of mirth;

Life there, welling, flowing,
  Waving round;
Pictures coming, going,
  Without sound.

Quick now! be this airy
  Globe repelled.
Never can the fairy
  Star be held.

Touched—it in a twinkle
  Disappears!
Leaving but a sprinkle
  As of tears.

A RIDDLE

What I say you'll scarce believe,
Yet my words shall not deceive;
I saw what seemed a little boy,
With a face of life and joy;
He danced, he ran, he nodded, he smiled,
Just like any other child;
But could not speak (how strange was this!)
Or cry, or breathe, nor could I kiss,
To save my life, the cherry red
Of lips, not living and not dead!
He was no picture, statue, doll;
He was not a child at all;
He was nothing, as near as could be,
He was as real as you or me.
. . . There he is: turn and see!

PLAYMATES AND PETS

I LOVE YOU, DEAR

I love you, Dear, I love you, Dear,
You can't think how I love you, Dear!
  Supposing I
  Were a butterfly
I'd waver around and above you, Dear.

A long way off I spied you, Dear,
No bonnet or hat could hide you, Dear;
  If I were a bird,
  Believe my word,
I'd sing every day beside you, Dear.

When you're away I miss you, Dear,
And now you're here I'll kiss you, Dear,
   And beg you will take
   This flower for my sake,
And my love along with this, you Dear!

CP

HERE AND THERE

(A Juvenile Chorus)

Where's Lucy?   Where's Lucy?
Far, far in the wood,
With wild birds for playmates,
And beech nuts for food.

No, here she is, here she is!
Happy and gay;
With singing and ringing,
To join in our lay!

Where's Gerald? Where's Gerald?
  He's out in the snow;
The stars shining keenly,
  The cold wind doth blow.

    No, here he is! here he is!
      Happy and gay;
    With singing and ringing,
      To join in our lay!

Where's Evey? Where's Evey?
  She's lost in the fog;
Go seek her, go find her,
  With man and with dog.

    No, here she is, here she is!
      Happy and gay;
    With singing and ringing,
      To join in our lay!

39

Where's Henry?   Where's Henry?
  Poor Henry's afloat;
The sea waves all round him,
  High tossing his boat.

        No, here he is! here he is!
          Happy and gay;
        With singing and ringing,
          To join in our lay!

Where's Charley? Where's Charley?
  In China dwells he;
He wears a long pigtail,
  Perpetually drinks tea.

     No, here he is! here he is!
      Happy and gay;
    With singing and ringing,
     To join in our lay!

41

Where's Johnny? Where's Johnny?
　　In Nubia, I know;
He has climbed a tall palm tree——
　　A lion's below.

　　　　No, here he is! here he is!
　　　　　　Happy and gay;
　　　　With singing and ringing,
　　　　　　To join in our lay!

Where's Mary? Where's Mary?
  Young Mary's asleep;
And round her white pillow
  The little dreams creep.

      No, here she is, here she is!
        Happy and gay;
      With singing and ringing,
        To join in our lay!

Where's Bertha? Where's Bertha?
  She has wings—she can fly!
She has flown to the bright moon——
  Look up there and spy!

    No, here she is, here she is!
     Happy and gay;
    With singing and ringing,
     To join in our lay!
     (*Ad infinitum*)

A MOUNTAIN ROUND

Take hands, merry neighbors, for dancing the
    round!
  Moonlight is fair and delicious the air;
From valley to valley our music shall sound,
  And startle the wolf in his lair.
From summits of snow to the forest below,
  Let vulture and crow hear the echoes, o-ho!
    (o-ho!)
While shadow on meadow in dancing the
    round
  Goes whirligig, pair after pair!

JINGLE, JANGLE

Jingle, jangle!
Riot and wrangle!
What shall we do
With people like you?
Here's Jingle!
There's Jangle!
Here's Riot!
There's Wrangle!
Never was seen such a turbulent crew!

You, north must go
To a hut of snow;
You, south in a trice,
To an island of spice;
You, off to Persia
And sit on a hill;
You, to that chair
And be five minutes still!

A CITY OF SAND

The sea! as smooth as silk,
And the froth of it like new milk,
And the sky of a wonderful blue——
The cliff harebells have it, too——
And scattered all over the shore
A thousand children or more!

Suppose we join, one-willed,
A city of sand to build,
With a rampart broad and strong
From rock to rock along,
Solid and firm enough
To last till the sea grows rough
And the days turn chilly and short,
The end of our seaside sport,
When all must bundle and pack
And swift in the train go back,
Big folk and little folk,
To London lamps and smoke?

Let's draw out our plan tonight,
Begin it with morning light,
We'll bring all the children together
And build in the sweet sunny weather.
What use in a house of sand?
But a city—that *would* be grand!
Oh, yes! I am sure it will stand!
And I, who first thought of the thing,
Perhaps they will make me king?

YES OR NO?

Yes or no?
Stay or go?
He never can tell, he never will know!
We must not wait,
We'll all be late,
While Barnaby puzzles his queer little pate!

What do you say?
Off and away!
Make up your mind to go or to stay.
Fix on your plan,
Step out like a man,
And follow your nose as fast as you can!

THE BIRD

"Birdie, Birdie! will you pet?
Summer-time is far away yet,
You'll have silken quilts and a velvet bed,
And a pillow of satin for your head!"

"I'd rather sleep in the ivy wall;
No rain comes through, tho' I hear it fall;
The sun peeps gay at dawn of day,
And I sing and wing away, away!"

"O Birdie, Birdie! will you pet?
Diamond stones and amber and jet
We'll string for a necklace fair and fine
To please this pretty bird of mine!"

"Oh, thanks for diamonds, and thanks for jet,
And here is something daintier yet——
A feather necklace round and round,
That I wouldn't sell for a thousand pound!"

"O Birdie, Birdie! won't you pet?
We'll buy you a dish of silver fret,
A golden cup and an ivory seat,
And carpets soft beneath your feet!"

"Can running water be drunk from gold?
Can a silver dish the forest hold?
A rocking twig is the finest chair,
And the softest paths lie through the air——
Goodbye, goodbye to my lady fair!"

ROBIN REDBREAST

Goodbye, goodbye to Summer!
  For Summer's nearly done;
The garden smiling faintly,
  Cool breezes in the sun;
Our thrushes now are silent,
  Our swallows flown away——
But Robin's here, in coat of brown,
  With ruddy breast-knot gay.
Robin, Robin Redbreast,
  O Robin dear!
Robin singing sweetly
  In the falling of the year.

Bright yellow, red, and orange,
  The leaves come down in hosts;
The trees are Indian princes,
  But soon they'll turn to ghosts;
The scanty pears and apples
  Hang russet on the bough,
It's Autumn, Autumn, Autumn late,
  'Twill soon be Winter now.
Robin, Robin Redbreast,
  O Robin dear!
And wellaway, my Robin,
  For pinching times are near!

The fireside for the cricket,
  The wheatstack for the mouse,
When trembling night-winds whistle
  And moan all round the house;
The frosty ways like iron,
  The branches plumed with snow——
Alas! in Winter dead and dark,
  Where can poor Robin go?

Robin, Robin Redbreast,
  O Robin dear!
And a crumb of bread for Robin,
  His little heart to cheer.

BIRDS' NAMES

Of creatures with feathers, come let us see
Which have names like you and me.
Hook-nosed Poll, that thinks herself pretty,
Every one knows, of all birds most witty.
Friendly Daw, in suit of gray,
Ask him his name, and "Jack!" he'll say.
Pert Philip Sparrow hopping you'll meet——
"Philip! Philip!"—in garden and street.
Bold Robin Redbreast perches near,
And sings his best in the fall of the year.

Grave Madge Owlet shuns the light,
And shouts "Hoo! hoo!" in the woods at
 night.
Nightingale sweet, that May loves well,
Old poets have called her Philomel,
But Philomelus, *he* sings best,
While *she* sits listening in her nest.
Darting Martin!—tell me why
They call you Martin. I know not, I;
Martin the black, under cottage eaves,
Martin the small, in sandy caves.

Merry Willy Wagtail, what runs he takes!
Wherever he stops, his tail he shakes.
Head and tail little Jenny Wren perks,
As in and out of the hedge she jerks.
Brisk Tom Tit, the lover of trees,
Picks off every fly and grub he sees.
Mag, the cunning chattering pie,
Builds her home in a treetop high——
Mag, you're a terrible thief— Oh, fie!

Tom and Philip and Jenny and Polly,
Madge and Martin and Robin and Willy,
Philomelus and friendly Jack——
Mag the rogue, half white, half black,
Stole an egg from every bird;
Such an uproar was never heard;
All of them flew upon Mag together,
And plucked her naked of every feather.
"You're not a bird!" they told her then,
"You may go away and live among men!"

FAIRIES AND ELVES

THE FAIRIES

Up the airy mountain,
　Down the rushy glen,
We daren't go a-hunting
　For fear of little men;
Wee folk, good folk,
　Trooping all together;
Green jacket, red cap,
　And white owl's feather!

Down along the rocky shore
　Some make their home,
They live on crispy pancakes
　Of yellow tide-foam;
Some in the reeds
　Of the black mountain-lake,
With frogs for their watch-dogs,
　All night awake.

High on the hilltop
　The old King sits;
He is now so old and gray
　He's nigh lost his wits.
With a bridge of white mist
　Columbkill he crosses,
On his stately journeys,
　From Slieveleague to Rosses;
Or going up with music
　On cold starry nights,
To sup with the Queen
　Of the gay Northern Lights.

They stole little Bridget
    For seven years long;
When she came down again
    Her friends were all gone.
They took her lightly back,
    Between the night and morrow,
They thought that she was fast asleep,
    But she was dead with sorrow.
They have kept her ever since
    Deep within the lake,
On a bed of flag-leaves,
    Watching till she wake.

By the craggy hillside
    Through the mosses bare,
They have planted thorn-trees
    For pleasure here and there.
Is any man so daring
    As dig them up in spite,
He shall find their sharpest thorns
    In his bed at night.

Up the airy mountain,
  Down the rushy glen,
We daren't go a-hunting
  For fear of little men;
Wee folk, good folk,
  Trooping all together;
Green jacket, red cap,
  And white owl's feather!

THE FAIRY KING

High on the hill-top
The old King sits;
He is now so old and gray
He's nigh lost his wits.

The Fairy King was old.
He met the Witch of the wold.
"Ah, ha, King!" quoth she,
"Now thou art old like me."
"Nay, Witch!" quoth he,
"I am not old like thee."

The King took off his crown,
It almost bent him down;
His age was too great
To carry such a weight.
"Give it here!" she said,
And clapt it on her head.

Crown sank to ground;
The Witch no more was found.
Then sweet spring-songs were sung,
The Fairy King grew young,
His crown was made of flowers,
He lived in woods and bowers.

THE ELF SINGING

An Elf sat on a twig,
He was not very big,
He sang a little song,
He did not think it wrong;
But he was on a Wizard's ground,
Who hated all sweet sound.

Elf, Elf,
Take care of yourself,
He's coming behind you,
To seize you and bind you
And stifle your song.
The Wizard! the Wizard!
He changes his shape
In crawling along,
An ugly old ape,
A poisonous lizard,
A spotted spider,
A wormy glider,
The Wizard! the Wizard!
He's up on the bough,
He'll bite through your gizzard,
He's close to you now!

The Elf went on with his song,
It grew more clear and strong,
  It lifted him into air,
    He floated singing away,
  With rainbows in his hair;
While the Wizard-worm from his creep
  Made a sudden leap,
  Fell down into a hole,
And, ere his magic word he could say,
  Was eaten up by a Mole.

CHORUS OF FAIRIES

Golden, golden,
Light unfolding,
Busily, merrily, work and play,
In flowery meadows
And forest shadows,
All the length of a Summer day!
All the length of a Summer day!

Sprightly, lightly,
Sing we rightly,
Moments brightly hurry away;
Fruit-tree blossoms
And roses' bosoms——
Clear blue sky of a Summer day!
Dear blue sky of a Summer day!

Springlets, brooklets,
Greeny nooklets,
Hill and valley and salt-sea spray,
Comrade rovers,
Fairy lovers——
All the length of a Summer day!
All the livelong Summer day!

THE FAIRY SHOE-MAKER

Little Cowboy, what have you heard,
　Up on the lonely rath's green mound?
Only the plaintive yellow bird
　Sighing in sultry fields around,
Chary, chary, chary, chee-ee!——
Only the grasshopper and the bee?——
　　　"Tip-tap, rip-rap,
　　　　Tick-a-tack-too!
　　　Scarlet leather sewn together,
　　　　This will make a shoe.
　　　Left right, pull it tight;
　　　　Summer days are warm;
　　　Underground in winter,
　　　　Laughing at the storm!"

Rath, an old fort or fortified house.
Yellow bird, the yellow bunting or "yorlin."

78

Lay your ear close to the hill.
  Do you not catch the tiny clamor,
  Busy click of an elfin hammer,
Voice of the Lepracaun singing shrill
As he merrily plies his trade?
  He's a span
  And a quarter in height.
Get him in sight, hold him tight,
  And you're a made Man!

II

You watch your cattle the summer day,
Sup on potatoes, sleep in the hay;
  How would you like to roll in your carriage,
  Look for a duchess's daughter in marriage?
Seize the Shoemaker—then you may!
    "Big boots a-hunting,
      Sandals in the hall,
    White for a wedding-feast,
      Pink for a ball.
    This way, that way,
      So we make a shoe;
    Getting rich every stitch,
      Tick-tack-too!"

Nine-and-ninety treasure crocks
This keen miser-fairy hath,
Hid in mountains, woods, and rocks,
And where the cormorants build;
      From times of old
      Guarded by him;
      Each of them filled
      Full to the brim
        With gold!

III

I caught him at work one day, myself,
  In the castle - ditch where foxglove
    grows——
A wrinkled, wizened, and bearded Elf,
  Spectacles stuck on his pointed nose,
  Silver buckles to his hose,
Leather apron—shoe in his lap——
     "Rip-rap, tip-tap,
      Tack-tack-too!
      (A green cricket on my cap!
      Away the moth flew!)
      Buskins for a fairy prince,
      Brogues for his son——
      Pay me well, pay me well,
      When the job is done!"

The rogue was mine, beyond a doubt,
  I stared at him, he stared at me;
  "Servant, Sir! Humph!" says he,
And pulled a snuff-box out.
He took a long pinch, looked better pleased,
The queer little Lepracaun;
  Offered the box with a whimsical grace—
  Pouf! he flung the dust in my face,
And, while I sneezed,
      Was gone!

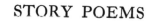

STORY POEMS

THE CAT AND THE DOG

There once lived a Man, a Cat, and a Dog,
And the Man built a house with stone and log.
"If you'll help to take care of this house with
     me,
One indoors, one out, your places must be."
Said both together, "Indoors I'll stay!"
And they argued the matter for half-a-day.

"Come, let us sing for it!" purrs the Cat;
"No!" barks the Dog, "I won't do that."
"Come let us fight for it!" growls Bow-wow;
"Nay!" says Pussy, "mee-ow, mee-ow!"
"Well, let us race for it!"—said and done.
The course is marked out, and away they run.

Puss bounded off; the Dog ran fast;
Quickly was Puss overtaken and pass'd;
But a Beggar who under the hedge did lie
Struck the poor Dog as he galloped by
A blow with his staff, and lessened his pace
To a limp; so Pussy won the race.

The Beggar went on his way to beg;
Dog was cured of his limping leg;
And Cat keeps the inside of the house,
Watching it well from rat and mouse,
Dog keeps the outside, ever since then,
And always barks at beggar-men.

NICK SPENCE

Nick Spence, Nick Spence,
Sold the Cow for sixpence!
　　When his Master scolded him,
　　　Nicky didn't care.
Put him in the farmyard,
The stableyard, the stackyard,
　　Send him to the pigsty,
　　　And Johnny to the fair!

RIDING

His Lordship's Steed
Of a noble breed
Is trotting it fleetly, fleetly,
Her Ladyship's pony,
Sleek and bony,
Cantering neatly, neatly.

How shall they pass
The Turf-Cadger's Ass,
Creels and all, creels and all?
Man on him bumping,
Shouting and thumping,
Heels and all, heels and all!

Lane is not wide,
A hedge on each side,
The Ass is beginning to bray;
  "Now," says my Lord,
  With an angry word,
"Fellow, get out of the way!"

  "Ha!" says the Cadger,
  As bold as a badger,
"This way is *my* way, too!"
  Says the Lady mild,
  And sweetly smiled,
"My Friend, that's perfectly true!"

The Cadger looked round,
Then jumped to the ground,
And into the hedge pulled Neddy.
"Oh, thank you!" says she,
"Ax pardon!" says he,
And touched his old hat to the Lady.

His Lordship's Steed
Of a noble breed
Went trotting it fleetly, fleetly,
Her Ladyship's pony,
Sleek and bony,
Cantering neatly, neatly.

The Cadger he rode
As well as he could,
Heels and all, heels and all,
Jolting and bumping,
Shouting and thumping,
Creels and all, creels and all.

TOM CRICKET

Tom Cricket he sat in his hole in the wall,
   Close to the kitchen fire;
Up and down ran the Cockroaches all,
Red coats and black coats, great and small.
"Ho, Tom; our hearts are set on a ball,
   And your music we desire!"

Tom sat in his hole, his horns hung out,
    He played away on his fiddle;
The Cockroaches danced in a rabble rout,
Scrambling and scurrying all about,
Tho' they had their own steps and figures no
    doubt,
    Hands across, and down the middle.

Till, "Stay!" says a Fat One, "We're no Elves,
    To dance all night without stopping!
Now for supper!" They helped themselves,
For the servants were gone to bed; on shelves
And tables they quested by tens and twelves,
    And quick to the floor kept dropping.

As a Cockroach ran by, says Tom Cricket to
    him,
  "Fetch me up a piece of potato,
Good Sir !—to mix in the crowd I'm too slim."
Says Jack Cockroach, "I see you are proud
    and prim;
To eat alone is merely your whim——
  Which I never will give way to !"

"Come down," says he, "and look out for
    your share !"
  "I won't do that," says Tom Cricket.
And when for another dance they care,
And call upon Tom for a lively air,
They find he has drawn himself back in his
    lair.
  "How shameful," they cry, "How wicked !"

"Let's fill up the mouth of his cave with soot,
  Because he's behaved so badly!"
They ran up and down the wall to do't;
But ere half-done—a dreadful salute!
In came the Cook, and the Scullion to boot,
  And off they all scampered madly.

THE FRIENDLY WORLD

THE BALL

All men, black, brown, red, yellow, white,
Are brethren in their Father's sight.
To do each other good is right,
But not to wrangle, steal, or fight.

A thousand millions, young and old,
Some in the heat, some in the cold,
Upon this Ball of Earth are rolled
Around the Sun's great flame of gold.

And this great Sun is like indeed
One daisy in a daisied mead;
For God's power doth all thought exceed.
And of us also He takes heed.

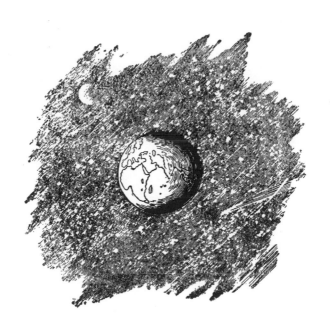

SEASONS

In Spring-time, the Forest,
In Summer, the Sea,
In Autumn, the Mountains,
In Winter—ah me!

How gay, the old branches
  A-swarm with new buds,
The primrose and bluebell
  Fresh-blown in the woods,
All green things unfolding,
  Where merry birds sing!
I love in the Woodlands
  To wander in Spring.

What joy, when the Sea-waves,
  In mirth and in might,
Spread purple in shadow,
  Flash white into light!
The gale fills the sail,
  And the gull flies away;
In crimson and gold
  Sets the long Summer day.

O pride! on the Mountains
   To leave earth below;
The great slopes of heather,
   One broad purple glow;
The loud-roaring torrent
   Leaps, bound after bound,
To plains of gold Autumn,
   With mist creeping round.

Ah, Wind, is it Winter?
   Yes, Winter is here;
With snow on the meadow,
   And ice on the mere.
The daylight is short,
   But the firelight is long;
Our skating's good sport;
   Then story and song.

In Spring-time, the Forest,
    In Summer, the Sea,
In Autumn, the Mountains——
    And Winter has glee.

DOWN ON THE SHORE

Down on the shore, on the sunny shore!
  Where the salt smell cheers the land;
Where the tide moves bright under bound-
    less light,
  And the surge on the glittering strand;
Where the children wade in the shallow pools,
  Or run from the froth in play;
While the swift little boats with milk-white
    wings
  Are crossing the sapphire bay,
And the ship in full sail, with a fortunate gale
  Holds proudly on her way;
Where the nets are spread on the grass to
    dry,
And asleep, hard by, the fishermen lie,
Under the tent of the warm blue sky,
With the hushing wave on its golden floor
    To sing their lullaby.